Word Problems for Model Drawing Practice

Level 1

Word Problems for Model Drawing Practice

Level 1

by Catherine Jones Kuhns

Peterborough, New Hampshire

Published by Crystal Springs Books
A division of Staff Development for Educators (SDE)

To reorder, please contact us at:
10 Sharon Road, PO Box 500
Peterborough, NH 03458
1-800-321-0401
www.SDE.com/crystalsprings

Published 2009
Printed in the United States of America
13 12 11 3 4 5

ISBN: 978-1-934026-24-3

Editor: Sharon Smith
Art Director and Designer: S. Dunholter
Production Coordinator: Deborah Fredericks

Contents

A Note to the Teacher

Each simple story problem in this workbook is designed to provide practice with one specific aspect of model drawing. The problems appear to be simple, and many of them could be solved—sometimes more quickly—in other ways. However, as we know, children need repeated practice with any concept, method, or strategy in order to internalize it. For that reason, the problems incorporate strategies that gradually progress in complexity, and they truly build upon one another. If you take the time to move through the problems slowly, your students will have a chance to practice each strategy and build confidence with it before moving on to another, more difficult one. As a result, they will develop a deep understanding of model drawing.

Model drawing is an incredibly powerful strategy, and like most things, it is most effective when it's taught incrementally. Once your children are able to read words and know how to follow along in choral reading, I encourage you to use just one of these problems a day. Don't hesitate to read the problem a few times with your young students. They will enjoy the extra practice, as some of the words will be new to them. Follow the steps in the order given in the directions. Discuss with your students what the steps are, how they work, and why they are helpful. Capitalize on the ways your students solve the problem, pointing out that often two students may reach the same correct answer in different ways. As you always do in your mathematics classes, encourage mathematical discussion and ask children to justify their answers.

As your students work with each type of problem, they will gain confidence and comfort with a particular strategy while mastering the skills they need to progress to the next level. And that means that one step at a time, one problem at a time, you will be creating the problem solvers we all want our students to be.

Catherine Jones Kuhns

1. Beginning Model Drawing

1. Chelsea picked 3 flowers.
Fran picked 4 flowers.
How many flowers did they pick in all?

(a) Fill in the numbers.

Chelsea's flowers ___

?

Fran's flowers ___

(b) Count the flowers or add.

3 + 4 = ___

(c) Write the answer next to the **?.** *Circle the answer.*

(d) Complete the sentence to answer the question.

They picked ___ flowers in all.

(e) Check: Does your answer make sense?

2. Joey has 3 goldfish.
Sasha has 5 goldfish.
How many fish do they have in all?

(a) Fill in the numbers.

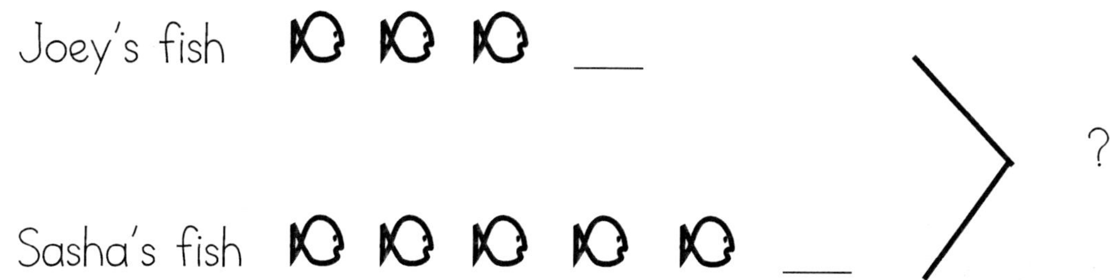

(b) Count the fish or add.

3 + 5 = ___

(c) Write the answer next to the **?***. Circle the answer.*

(d) Complete the sentence to answer the question.

They have ___ fish in all.

(e) Check: Does your answer make sense?

3. Simone read 6 books.
Albert read 4 books.
How many books did they read in all?

(a) Fill in the numbers and the **?***.*

Simone's books 📖📖📖📖📖📖 ___

Albert's books 📖📖📖📖 ___

> ___

(b) Count or add.

6 + 4 = ___

(c) Write the answer next to the **?***. Circle the answer.*

(d) Complete the sentence to answer the question.

They read ___ books in all.

(e) Does your answer make sense?

4. Jenny has 7 crayons.
Sidney has 3 crayons.
How many crayons do they have in all?

(a) Fill in the numbers and the **?**.

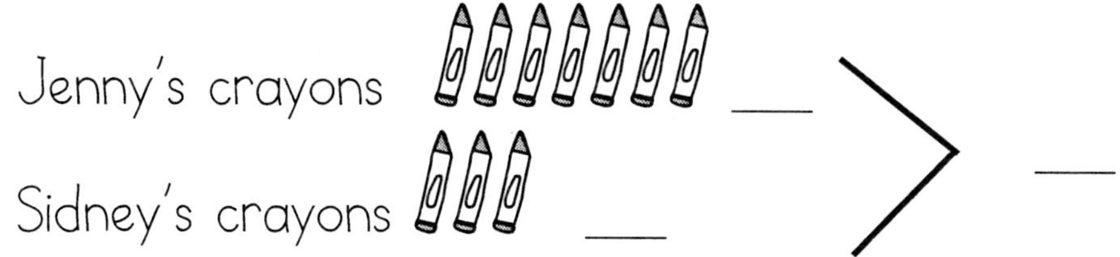

(b) Count or add.

7 + 3 = ___

(c) Write the answer next to the **?***. Circle the answer.*

(d) Write the number in the sentence.

They have ___ crayons in all.

(e) Does your answer make sense?

5. Terry scored 4 baskets.
Olivia scored 5 baskets.
How many baskets did they score in all?

(a) Fill in the numbers and the **?***.*

Terry's baskets  ___

Olivia's baskets  ___

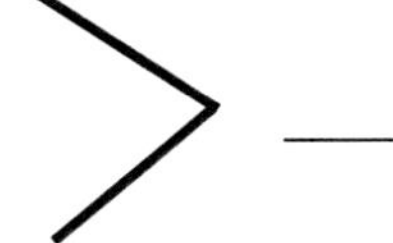 ___

(b) Count or add.

4 + 5 = ___

(c) Write the answer next to the **?***. Circle the answer.*

(d) Write the number in the sentence.

They scored ___ baskets in all.

(e) Does your answer make sense?

6. Mavis ate 5 candy hearts.
Arturo ate 7 candy hearts.
How many hearts did they eat in all?

(a) Fill in the numbers from the problem.
(b) Add the **?***.*
(c) Add or count the hearts. Fill in the blank after the equal sign.
(d) Write the answer next to the **?***. Circle the answer.*
(e) Complete the sentence.

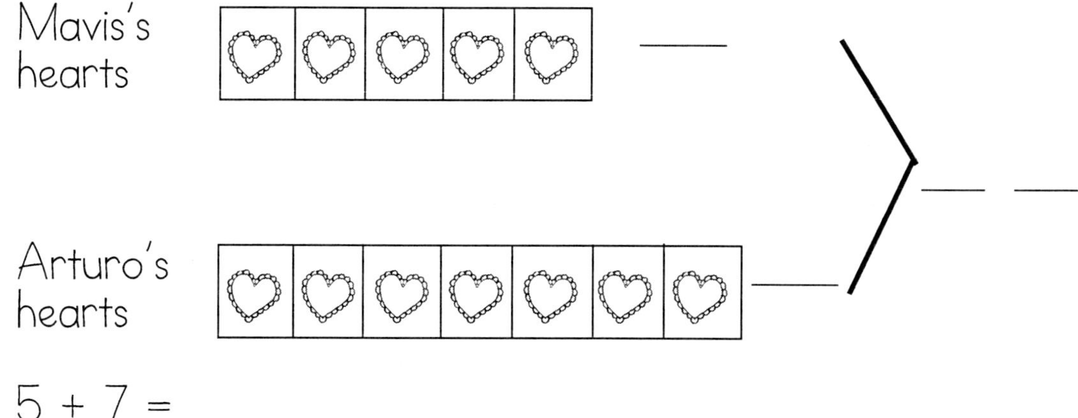

5 + 7 = ___

They ate ___ hearts in all.

7. Henry scored 5 goals.
Jerri scored 5 goals.
How many goals did they score?

(a) Fill in the numbers from the problem.
(b) Add the **?**.
(c) Add or count the goals. Fill in the blank after the equal sign.
(d) Write the answer next to the **?**. *Circle the answer.*
(e) Complete the sentence.

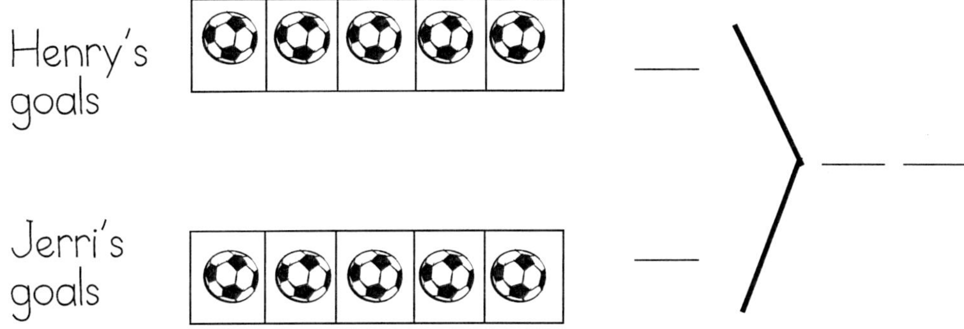

5 + 5 = ___

They scored ___ goals.

8. Bob painted 7 boats.
Torrie painted 4 boats.
How many boats did they paint in all?

(a) Fill in the numbers from the problem.
(b) Add the **?**.
(c) Add or count the boats. Fill in the blank after the equal sign.
(d) Write the answer next to the **?**. *Circle the answer.*
(e) Complete the sentence.

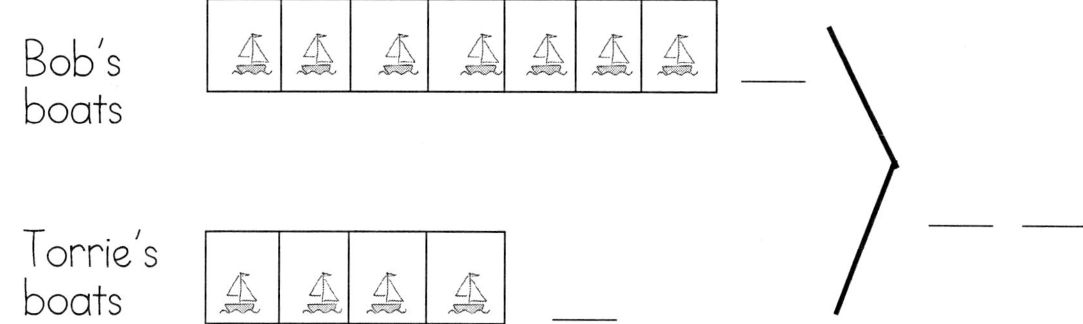

7 + 4 = ___

They painted ___ boats in all.

9. Joe flew 3 kites.
Sam flew 7 kites.
How many kites did the boys fly?

(a) Fill in the numbers from the problem.
(b) Add the **?**.
(c) Add or count the kites. Fill in the blank after the equal sign.
(d) Write the total number of kites next to the **?**. *Circle that number.*
(e) Complete the sentence.

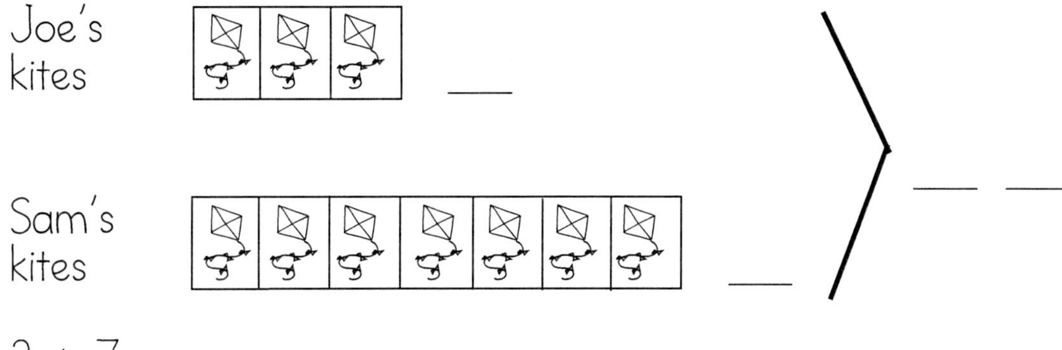

3 + 7 = ___

The boys flew ___ kites.

10. Alex has 4 cars.
Ty has 6 cars.
How many cars do the boys have in all?

(a) Fill in the numbers from the problem.
(b) Add the **?**.
(c) Add or count the cars. Fill in the blank after the equal sign.
(d) Write the total number of cars next to the **?**. *Circle that number.*
(e) Complete the sentence.

Alex's cars ___

Ty's cars ___

___ ___

4 + 6 = ___

They have ___ cars in all.

11. Danny counted 3 dogs.
David counted 6 dogs.
How many dogs did they count in all?

(a) Fill in the numbers from the problem.
(b) Add a ***bracket****.*
(c) Add the **?**.
(d) Add or count the ***unit bars****.*
(e) Write the answer next to the **?**. *Circle the answer.*
(f) Complete the sentence.

Danny's dogs ___

David's dogs ___

___ ___

They counted ___ dogs in all.

12. Julio caught 4 fish.
Marco caught 6 fish.
How many fish did they catch in all?

(a) Fill in the numbers from the problem.
(b) Add a bracket.
(c) Add the **?***.*
(d) Add or count the unit bars.
(e) Write the answer next to the **?***. Circle the answer.*
(f) Complete the sentence.

Julio's fish ___

Marco's fish ___

___ ___

They caught ___ fish in all.

13. Lo found 6 pennies.
John found 4 pennies.
How many pennies did they find in all?

(a) Fill in the numbers from the problem.
(b) Add a bracket.
(c) Add the **?***.*
(d) Add or count the unit bars.
(e) Write the answer next to the **?***. Circle the answer.*
(f) Complete the sentence.

Lo's pennies ___

John's pennies ___

___ ___

They found ___ pennies in all.

14. Michael shot 4 baskets.
Nick shot 5 baskets.
How many baskets did the boys shoot in all?

(a) Fill in the numbers from the problem.
(b) Add a bracket.
(c) Add the **?**.
(d) Add or count the unit bars.
(e) Write the answer next to the **?**. *Circle the answer.*
(f) Complete the sentence.

Michael's baskets	☐☐☐☐	___	
Nick's baskets	☐☐☐☐☐	___	___ ___

They shot ___ baskets in all.

15. Lu kicked 8 soccer goals.
Mia kicked 9 soccer goals.
How many goals did they kick in all?

(a) Fill in the numbers from the problem.
(b) Add a bracket.
(c) Add the **?**.
(d) Add or count the unit bars.
(e) Write the answer next to the ?. Circle the answer.
(f) Complete the sentence.

Lu's goals	☐☐☐☐☐☐☐☐	___	
Mia's goals	☐☐☐☐☐☐☐☐☐	___	___ ___

They kicked ____ goals in all.

16. Rover chewed 7 sticks.
Bowser chewed 9 sticks.
How many sticks did they chew in all?

(a) Draw the unit bars.
(b) Add the numbers from the problem, a bracket, and a **?***.*
(c) Add or count the unit bars.
(d) Write the answer next to the **?***. Circle the answer.*
(e) Complete the sentence.

Rover's sticks

Bowser's sticks

Rover and Bowser chewed ___ sticks in all.

17. Fluffy sleeps on 5 balls of yarn.
Puffy sleeps on 8 balls of yarn.
How many balls of yarn do the kittens need?

(a) Draw the unit bars.
(b) Add the numbers from the problem, a bracket, and a **?***.*
(c) Add or count the unit bars.
(d) Write the answer next to the **?***. Circle the answer.*
(e) Complete the sentence.

Fluffy's yarn

Puffy's yarn

The kittens need ___ balls of yarn.

18. Emily blew 9 bubbles.
Jeremy blew 9 bubbles.
How many bubbles did they blow in all?

(a) Draw the unit bars.
(b) Add the numbers from the problem, a bracket, and a ?.
(c) Add or count the unit bars.
(d) Write the answer next to the ?. Circle the answer.
(e) Complete the sentence.

Emily's bubbles

Jeremy's bubbles

They blew ___ bubbles in all.

19. Damian painted 9 pictures.
Haley painted 7 pictures.
Enrique painted 5 pictures.
How many pictures did they paint in all?

(a) Draw the unit bars.
(b) Add the numbers from the problem, a bracket, and a ?.
(c) Add or count the unit bars.
(d) Write the answer next to the ?. Circle the answer.
(e) Complete the sentence.

Damian's pictures

Haley's pictures

Enrique's pictures

They painted ___ pictures in all.

20. Hannah ate 3 mints.
Julia ate 3 mints.
Ted ate 4 mints.
How many mints did they eat in all?

(a) Draw the unit bars.
(b) Add the numbers from the problem, a bracket, and a ?.
(c) Add or count the unit bars.
(d) Write the answer next to the ?. Circle the answer.
(e) Complete the sentence.

Hannah's mints

Julia's mints

Ted's mints

They ate ___ mints in all.

21. Adam ate 7 strawberries.
Peter ate 8 strawberries.
Marco ate 5 strawberries.
How many strawberries did the boys eat in all?

(a) Draw the unit bars.
(b) Add the numbers from the problem, a bracket, and a ?.
(c) Add or count the unit bars.
(d) Write the answer next to the ?. Circle the answer.
(e) Complete the sentence.

Adam's strawberries

Peter's strawberries

Marco's strawberries

The boys ate ___ strawberries in all.

22. Amanda has 5 cookies.
Sami has 4 cookies.
How many cookies do they have in all?

(a) Draw the unit bars.
(b) Add the numbers from the problem, a bracket, and a **?***.*
(c) Add or count the unit bars.
(d) Write the answer next to the **?***. Circle the answer.*
(e) Complete the sentence.

Amanda's cookies

Sami's cookies

The girls have ___ cookies in all.

2. One-Person Problems

23. Mario baked 5 pizzas in the afternoon and 6 pizzas in the evening. How many pizzas did he bake in all?

(a) Solve the problem.
(b) Fill in the blanks.

Mario's afternoon pizzas

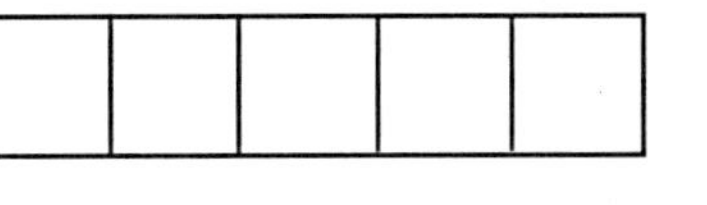

5

Mario's evening pizzas

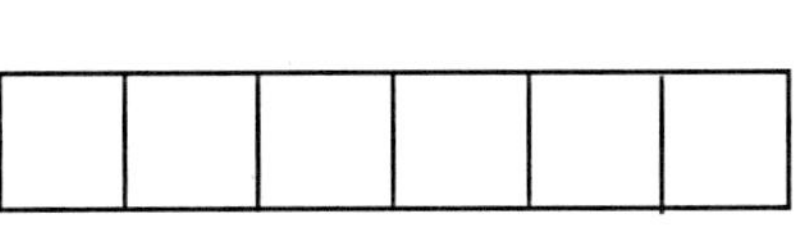

6

? ___

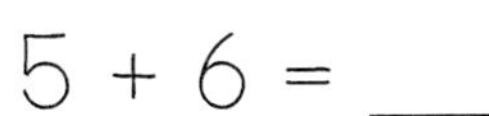

5 + 6 = ___

Mario baked ___ pizzas in all.

24. Kenny played the piano for 4 hours on Saturday and 3 hours on Sunday. How many hours did he play the piano over the weekend?

(a) Draw the unit bars.
(b) Add the numbers from the problem, a bracket, and a **?**.
(c) Add or count the unit bars.
(d) Write the answer next to the **?**. *Circle the answer.*
(e) Complete the sentence.

Kenny's Saturday hours

Kenny's Sunday hours

Kenny played the piano for ____ ______________ .

25. Luigi baked 6 batches of brownies on Saturday and 6 batches of brownies on Sunday. How many batches of brownies did Luigi bake on Saturday and Sunday?

(a) Draw the unit bars.
(b) Add the numbers from the problem, a bracket, and a **?**.
(c) Add or count the unit bars.
(d) Write the answer next to the **?**. *Circle the answer.*
(e) Complete the sentence.

Luigi's Saturday brownies

Luigi's Sunday brownies

Luigi baked ___ batches of ______________________ .

26. Janice baked 5 pies and 8 cakes last week. How many desserts did she bake in all?

(a) Draw the unit bars.
(b) Add the numbers from the problem, a bracket, and a **?**.
(c) Add or count the unit bars.
(d) Write the answer next to the **?**. *Circle the answer.*
(e) Complete the sentence.

Janice's pies

Janice's cakes

Janice baked _____ __________________ in all.

27. Meg strung 12 beads on her necklace and 8 beads on her bracelet. How many beads did Meg use?

(a) Draw the unit bars.
(b) Add the numbers from the problem, a bracket, and a **?**.
(c) Add or count the unit bars.
(d) Write the answer next to the **?**. *Circle the answer.*
(e) Complete the sentence.

Meg's necklace beads

Meg's bracelet beads

Meg used ____ ______________________ .

28. Jeremiah, the cook at the diner, grilled 6 hamburgers for lunch and 7 hamburgers for dinner. How many hamburgers did he grill?

(a) Draw the unit bars.
(b) Add the numbers from the problem, a bracket, and a **?**.
(c) Add or count the unit bars.
(d) Write the answer next to the **?**. *Circle the answer.*
(e) Complete the sentence.

Jeremiah's lunch hamburgers

Jeremiah's dinner hamburgers

Jeremiah grilled ____ ______________________ .

29. Franz pitched 4 fastballs and 8 slow balls. How many balls did Franz pitch in all?

(a) Draw the unit bars.
(b) Add the numbers from the problem, a bracket, and a **?**.
(c) Add or count the unit bars.
(d) Write the answer next to the **?**. *Circle the answer.*
(e) Complete the sentence.

Franz's fastballs

Franz's slow balls

Franz pitched ____ ________________________ .

30. The puppy chewed 5 old shoes and 6 new shoes. How many shoes did the puppy chew?

(a) Draw the unit bars.
(b) Add the numbers from the problem, a bracket, and a **?**.
(c) Add or count the unit bars.
(d) Write the answer next to the **?**. *Circle the answer.*
(e) Complete the sentence.

Old shoes

New shoes

The puppy chewed ____ ________________________ .

31. Maria served 5 plates of spaghetti and 7 plates of chicken. How many plates did Maria serve in all?

(a) Draw the unit bars.
(b) Add the numbers from the problem, a bracket, and a **?***.*
(c) Add or count the unit bars.
(d) Write the answer next to the **?***. Circle the answer.*
(e) Complete the sentence.

Maria's plates of spaghetti

Maria's plates of chicken

Maria served ____ ______________________________ .

32. Sergio wrapped 6 large gifts and 7 small gifts. How many gifts did Sergio wrap in all?

(a) Draw the unit bars.
(b) Add the numbers from the problem, a bracket, and a **?***.*
(c) Add or count the unit bars.
(d) Write the answer next to the **?***. Circle the answer.*
(e) Complete the sentence.

Sergio's large gifts

Sergio's small gifts

Sergio wrapped ____ ______________________________ in all.

33. Gabriella tossed 5 fruit salads and 6 veggie salads. How many salads did Gabriella toss?

(a) Draw the unit bars.
(b) Add the numbers from the problem, a bracket, and a **?**.
(c) Add or count the unit bars.
(d) Write the answer next to the **?**. *Circle the answer.*
(e) Complete the sentence.

Gabriella's
fruit salads

Gabriella's
veggie salads

Gabriella tossed _____ ______________________________ .

34. Mrs. Chen bought 4 pears and 7 apples. How many pieces of fruit did Mrs. Chen buy?

(a) Draw the unit bars.
(b) Add the numbers from the problem, a bracket, and a **?**.
(c) Add or count the unit bars.
(d) Write the answer next to the **?**. *Circle the answer.*
(e) Complete the sentence.

Mrs. Chen's pears

Mrs. Chen's apples

Mrs. Chen bought ___ pieces of ______________.

35. Lars bought 5 chocolate cookies and 7 oatmeal cookies. How many cookies did Lars buy?

(a) Draw the unit bars.
(b) Add the numbers from the problem, a bracket, and a **?**.
(c) Add or count the unit bars.
(d) Write the answer next to the **?**. *Circle the answer.*
(e) Complete the sentence.

Lars's chocolate cookies

Lars's oatmeal cookies

Lars bought ____ ____________________ .

36. The cook served 6 chicken dinners and 7 hamburger dinners. How many dinners did the cook serve?

(a) Draw the unit bars.
(b) Add the numbers from the problem, a bracket, and a **?**.
(c) Add or count the unit bars.
(d) Write the answer next to the **?**. *Circle the answer.*
(e) Complete the sentence.

Cook's chicken dinners

Cook's hamburger dinners

The cook served ____ ____________________ .

37. Claudia decorated 5 cakes on Tuesday, 7 cakes on Wednesday, and 4 cakes on Thursday. How many cakes did Claudia decorate in those 3 days?

(a) Draw the unit bars.
(b) Add the numbers from the problem, a bracket, and a **?***.*
(c) Add or count the unit bars.
(d) Write the answer next to the **?***. Circle the answer.*
(e) Complete the sentence.

Claudia's
Tuesday cakes

Claudia's
Wednesday cakes

Claudia's
Thursday cakes

Claudia decorated _____ ______________________________ .

3. Problems with Missing Numbers

38. Max found 8 shiny rocks. Fritz found the same number of rocks as Max. How many rocks do they have in all?

(a) Draw the unit bars.
(b) Add the numbers from the problem, plus a bracket and a **?**.
(c) Add or count the unit bars.
(d) Write the answer next to the **?**. *Circle the answer.*
(e) Complete the sentence.

Max's rocks

Fritz's rocks

The boys have ___ rocks in all.

39. Rachel read 7 books this summer. Her sister read 2 more books than Rachel. How many books did the girls read in all?

(a) Draw the unit bars.
(b) Add the numbers from the problem, plus brackets and a **?**.
(c) Add or count the unit bars.
(d) Write the answer next to the **?**. *Circle the answer.*
(e) Complete the sentence.

Rachel's books

Sister's books

The girls read ___ books in all.

40. Gino ran 7 miles on Saturday. On Sunday he ran 1 more mile than on Saturday. How many miles did he run over the weekend?

(a) Fill in the rest of the "what."
(b) Draw the unit bars.
(c) Add the numbers from the problem, plus brackets and a **?**.
(d) Add or count the unit bars.
(e) Write the answer next to the **?**. *Circle the answer.*
(f) Complete the sentence.

Gino's Saturday ______

Gino's Sunday ______

Gino ran _____ ________________________________ .

41. Emanuel had quarters and dimes. He had 8 quarters. He had one fewer dime than quarters. How many coins did Emanuel have?

(a) Draw the unit bars.
(b) Add the numbers from the problem, plus brackets and a **?**.
(c) Add or count the unit bars.
(d) Write the answer next to the **?**. *Circle the answer.*
(e) Complete the sentence.

Emanuel's quarters

Emanuel's dimes

Emanuel had _____ ________________________________ .

42. Martin caught 6 lightning bugs on Tuesday night. He caught 1 more lightning bug on Wednesday night than Tuesday night. How many lightning bugs did he catch in all?

(a) Fill in the rest of the "what."
(b) Draw the unit bars.
(c) Add the numbers from the problem, plus brackets and a **?***.*
(d) Solve the problem. Show your work.
(e) Write the answer next to the **?***. Circle the answer.*
(f) Complete the sentence.

Martin's
Tuesday

______________________ ______

Martin's
Wednesday

______________________ ______

Martin caught ___ ______________ _______ in all.

43. Lakisha ate 5 hot dogs at the fair. Simon ate 4 more hot dogs than Lakisha. How many hot dogs did they eat in all?

(a) Fill in the "what."
(b) Draw the unit bars.
(c) Add the numbers from the problem, plus brackets and a **?***.*
(d) Solve the problem. Show your work.
(e) Write the answer next to the **?***. Circle the answer.*
(f) Complete the sentence.

Lakisha's ______ ______

Simon's ______ ______

Lakisha and Simon ate ___ __________ ________ in all.

44. Min-Jung checked out 6 books at the library. Her sister, Yean-Joo, checked out 3 more books than Min-Jung. How many books did the sisters check out?

(a) Fill in the "what."
(b) Draw the unit bars.
(c) Add the numbers from the problem, plus brackets and a **?**.
(d) Solve the problem. Show your work.
(e) Write the answer next to the **?**. *Circle the answer.*
(f) Complete the sentence.

Min-Jung's ________

Yean-Joo's ________

The sisters checked out ___ ____________________ .

45. Mr. Cho has 7 tulips. He has 2 more daisies than tulips. How many flowers does he have in all?

(a) Fill in the "what."
(b) Draw the unit bars.
(c) Add the numbers from the problem, plus brackets and a **?**.
(d) Solve the problem. Show your work.
(e) Write the answer next to the **?**. *Circle the answer.*
(f) Complete the sentence.

Mr. Cho's ____________

Mr. Cho's ____________

He has ___ ________________________ in all.

46. Dennis has 7 yo-yos. His sister has 2 fewer yo-yos than Dennis. How many yo-yos do they have in all?

(a) Fill in the "what."
(b) Draw the unit bars.
(c) Add the numbers from the problem, plus brackets and a **?***.*
(d) Solve the problem. Show your work.
(e) Write the answer next to the **?***. Circle the answer.*
(f) Complete the sentence.

Dennis's ______ -______

Sister's ______-______

They have ___ ________________- __________ in all.

47. Lawrence collected 7 boxes of newspapers to recycle. Sabrina collected 4 boxes of newspapers more than Lawrence. How many boxes did they collect in all?

(a) Fill in the "what."
(b) Draw the unit bars.
(c) Add the numbers from the problem, plus brackets and a **?***.*
(d) Solve the problem. Show your work.
(e) Write the answer next to the **?***. Circle the answer.*
(f) Complete the sentence.

Lawrence's ______________

Sabrina's ______________

They collected ___ ____________________ in all.

48. Raquel swam for 6 hours this weekend. Mandy swam for 1 hour more than Raquel. How many hours did the girls swim?

(a) Fill in the "what."
(b) Draw the unit bars.
(c) Add the numbers from the problem, plus brackets and a **?**.
(d) Solve the problem. Show your work.
(e) Write the answer next to the **?**. *Circle the answer.*
(f) Complete the sentence.

Raquel's ______________

Mandy's ______________

The girls swam for ___ ____________________ .

4. Subtraction

49. Tom had 12 seashells in his bucket. Then 7 shells fell out. How many are left?

(a) Fill in the missing numbers in the drawing.
(b) Fill in the blank after the equal sign.
(c) Circle the answer next to the **?***.*
(d) Complete the sentence.

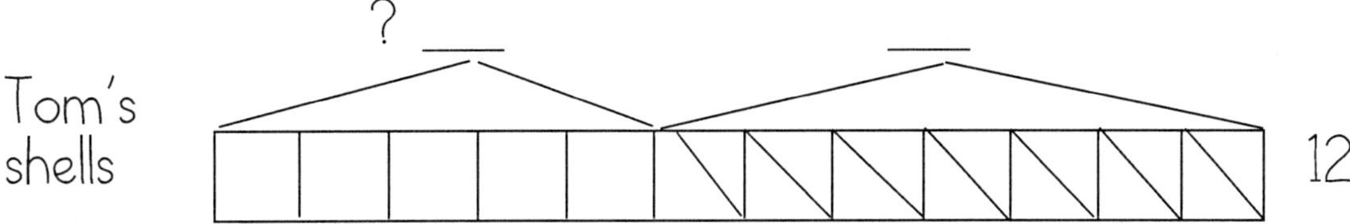

12 - 7 = ___

There are ___ shells left.

50. Sari had 9 buttons on her shirt. Oops! Two buttons popped off. How many buttons are left?

(a) Fill in the "what."
(b) Draw the unit bars.
(c) Write the numbers from the problem. Draw brackets and a **?***.*
(d) Solve the problem. Show your work.
(e) Write the answer next to the **?***. Circle the answer.*
(f) Complete the sentence.

Sari's ______________________

Sari has ___ buttons left.

51. Diego took 12 T-shirts to camp. When he came home, he forgot to pack 5 of those T-shirts. How many T-shirts does he have now?

(a) Fill in the "what."
(b) Draw the unit bars.
(c) Write the numbers from the problem. Draw brackets and a **?**.
(d) Solve the problem. Show your work.
(e) Write the answer next to the **?**. *Circle the answer.*
(f) Complete the sentence.

Diego's

____

Diego has _____ ________________________ now.

52. Ten rockets were on the launch pad. Then 8 rockets blasted into the air. How many rockets are left on the launch pad?

(a) Draw the unit bars.
(b) Write the numbers from the problem. Draw brackets and a **?**.
(c) Solve the problem. Show your work.
(d) Write the answer next to the **?**. *Circle the answer.*
(e) Complete the sentence.

Rockets

There are _____ ________________________ left on the launch pad.

53. Grandma baked 12 cookies. Aaron ate 8 of the cookies. How many cookies are left?

(a) Fill in the "what."
(b) Draw the unit bars.
(c) Write the numbers from the problem. Draw brackets and a **?***.*
(d) Solve the problem. Show your work.
(e) Write the answer next to the **?***. Circle the answer.*
(f) Complete the sentence.

Grandma's

____

There are _____ ______________________ left.

54. The baker had 11 loaves of bread. Sam bought 7 loaves. How many loaves of bread are left?

(a) Fill in the rest of the "what."
(b) Draw the unit bars.
(c) Write the numbers from the problem. Draw brackets and a **?***.*
(d) Solve the problem. Show your work.
(e) Write the answer next to the **?***. Circle the answer.*
(f) Complete the sentence.

Baker's

________ of __________

There are _____ ________________________________ of
_________________________ left.

55. Fritz had 13 baseball cards. He gave his brother 6 of his cards. How many cards does Fritz have now?

(a) Fill in the "what."
(b) Draw the unit bars.
(c) Write the numbers from the problem. Draw brackets and a **?***.*
(d) Solve the problem. Show your work.
(e) Write the answer next to the **?***. Circle the answer.*
(f) Complete the sentence.

Fritz's

____

______ has _______ ____________________ .

56. Rover had 10 bones. He hid 7 of the bones. How many bones did he not hide?

(a) Fill in the "what."
(b) Draw the unit bars.
(c) Write the numbers from the problem. Draw brackets and a **?***.*
(d) Solve the problem. Show your work.
(e) Write the answer next to the **?***. Circle the answer.*
(f) Complete the sentence.

Rover's

____

Rover did not hide ______ ____________________ .

57. Malik had 10 colored pencils in his backpack. Then 4 pencils fell out. How many pencils does he have now?

(a) Fill in the "what."
(b) Draw the unit bars.
(c) Write the numbers from the problem. Draw brackets and a **?**.
(d) Solve the problem. Show your work.
(e) Write the answer next to the **?**. *Circle the answer.*
(f) Complete the sentence.

Malik's

____

__________________ has _____ _______________ now.

58. Lauren had 11 pretzels in her lunch bag. She ate 6 pretzels. How many pretzels are left?

(a) Fill in the "what."
(b) Draw the unit bars.
(c) Write the numbers from the problem. Draw brackets and a **?**.
(d) Solve the problem. Show your work.
(e) Write the answer next to the **?**. *Circle the answer.*
(f) Complete the sentence.

Lauren's

____

__________________ has _____ _______________ left.

59. Gabby had 9 paintings in her folder, but 3 paintings fell out in the morning and 3 more paintings fell out in the afternoon. How many paintings does Gabby have in her folder now?

(a) Fill in the "what."
(b) Draw the unit bars.
(c) Write the numbers from the problem. Draw brackets and a ?.
(d) Solve the problem. Show your work.
(e) Write the answer next to the ?. Circle the answer.
(f) Complete the sentence.

Gabby's

____

__________________ has _____ ____________________

in her folder now.

60. Tyler had $10. He spent $2 at the school store and $3 at the ice cream store. How much money does Tyler have now?

(a) Fill in the "what."
(b) Draw the unit bars.
(c) Write the numbers from the problem. Draw brackets and a ?.
(d) Solve the problem. Show your work.
(e) Write the answer next to the ?. Circle the answer.
(f) Complete the sentence.

Tyler's

____

__________________ has _______ now.

61. Mr. Li had 12 cakes in the bakery. He sold 6 of the cakes. How many cakes does Mr. Li have in the bakery?

(a) Fill in the "what."
(b) Draw the unit bars.
(c) Write the numbers from the problem. Draw brackets and a **?**.
(d) Solve the problem. Show your work.
(e) Write the answer next to the **?**. *Circle the answer.*
(f) Complete the sentence.

Mr. Li's

____

______ ______ has ______ __________ in the bakery.

62. Kendall made 9 signs. She hung up 5 of the signs. How many signs does she have left to hang?

(a) Fill in the "what."
(b) Draw the unit bars.
(c) Write the numbers from the problem. Draw brackets and a **?**.
(d) Solve the problem. Show your work.
(e) Write the answer next to the **?**. *Circle the answer.*
(f) Complete the sentence.

Kendall's

____

________________ has ______ ________________ left to hang.

63. Mrs. Zhu made 12 eggrolls. Her family ate 9 of the eggrolls. How many eggrolls were left?

(a) Fill in the "what."
(b) Draw the unit bars.
(c) Write the numbers from the problem. Draw brackets and a **?**.
(d) Solve the problem. Show your work.
(e) Write the answer next to the **?**. *Circle the answer.*
(f) Complete the sentence.

Mrs. Zhu's

____

There were _____ __________________________ left.

64. Carol caught 11 lightning bugs and put them in a jar. She let 6 out of the jar. How many are left in the jar?

(a) Fill in the rest of the "what."
(b) Draw the unit bars.
(c) Write the numbers from the problem. Draw brackets and a **?**.
(d) Solve the problem. Show your work.
(e) Write the answer next to the **?**. *Circle the answer.*
(f) Complete the sentence.

Carol's lightning

____

There are ___ lightning bugs __________________ .

65. Chantelle had 11 apples. She fed 4 of the apples to the horses. How many apples did she have left?

(a) Fill in the "what."
(b) Draw the unit bars.
(c) Write the numbers from the problem. Draw brackets and a **?**.
(d) Solve the problem. Show your work.
(e) Write the answer next to the **?**. *Circle the answer.*
(f) Complete the sentence.

Chantelle's

____

Chantelle had ______ ________________ ________________.

5. Comparison Problems

66. Holly has 12 markers. Becca has 7 markers. What is the difference in the number of markers?

(a) Count how many more.
(b) Write the answer next to the **?**. *Circle the answer.*
(c) Complete the sentence.

Holly's markers 12

? ___

Becca's markers 7

Holly has ____ more markers than Becca.

67. Keith has 11 video games. Maddie has 14 video games. What is the difference in the number of their video games?

(a) Fill in the "what."
(b) Write the numbers from the problem. Draw a bracket and a **?**.
(c) Solve the problem.
(d) Write the answer next to the **?**. *Circle the answer.*
(e) Complete the sentence.

Keith's

____

Maddie's

____

Maddie has ________ more games than Keith.

68. Buzz knocked down 10 bowling pins. Sandy knocked down 4 pins. How many more pins did Buzz knock down than Sandy?

(a) Fill in the "what."
(b) Write the numbers from the problem. Draw a bracket and a **?***.*
(c) Solve the problem.
(d) Write the answer next to the **?***. Circle the answer.*
(e) Complete the sentence.

Buzz's

____

Sandy's

____

Buzz knocked down ___ more pins than Sandy.

69. Caryn has 13 key chains. Savannah has 8 key chains. What is the difference in the number of key chains the 2 girls have?

(a) Fill in the "what."
(b) Write the numbers from the problem. Draw a bracket and a **?***.*
(c) Solve the problem.
(d) Write the answer next to the **?***. Circle the answer.*
(e) Complete the sentence.

Caryn's

_________ _________

Savannah's

_________ _________

Caryn has ___ more _________ _________ than Savannah.

70. Corrie ate 12 jellybeans. Jason ate 8 jellybeans. What is the difference in the number of jellybeans the 2 ate?

(a) Fill in the "what."
(b) Write the numbers from the problem. Draw a bracket and a **?**.
(c) Solve the problem.
(d) Write the answer next to the **?**. *Circle the answer.*
(e) Complete the sentence.

Corrie's

____

Jason's

____

Corrie ate ___ _____ jellybeans than ________________.

71. There were 10 sailboats and 7 canoes in the water. How many more sailboats than canoes were there?

(a) Fill in the "what."
(b) Write the numbers from the problem. Draw a bracket and a **?**.
(c) Solve the problem.
(d) Write the answer next to the **?**. *Circle the answer.*
(e) Complete the sentence.

____

____

There were ___ more sailboats than ________________.

72. Mrs. Aziz has 14 roses and 9 daisies in a bouquet. How many more roses than daisies does Mrs. Aziz have?

(a) Fill in the "who" and the "what."
(b) Write the numbers from the problem. Draw a bracket and a **?**.
(c) Solve the problem.
(d) Write the answer next to the **?**. *Circle the answer.*
(e) Complete the sentence.

____

________ ________

____

________ ________

Mrs. Aziz has ______ more ____________ than daisies.

73. Clark won tic-tac-toe 10 times. Henri won tic-tac-toe 7 times. What is the difference in the number of tic-tac-toe wins for Clark and Henri?

(a) Fill in the "who" and the "what."
(b) Write the numbers from the problem. Draw a bracket and a **?**.
(c) Solve the problem.
(d) Write the answer next to the **?**. *Circle the answer.*
(e) Complete the sentence.

________ ________

________ ________

Clark won tic-tac-toe ___ more times than __________ .

74. Tia paid $13 for her video game and $4 for her book. What is the difference between the price of the video game and the price of the book?

(a) Fill in the "who" and the "what."
(b) Write the numbers from the problem. Draw a bracket and a **?**.
(c) Solve the problem.
(d) Write the answer next to the **?**. *Circle the answer.*
(e) Complete the sentence.

____

____

____

____

Tia's game cost _________ more

than her _________________.

75. Luis collects baseball and football cards. He has 9 boxes of baseball cards and 14 boxes of football cards. What is the difference in the number of his boxes of baseball and football cards?

(a) Fill in the "who" and the "what."
(b) Write the numbers from the problem. Draw a bracket and a **?**.
(c) Solve the problem.
(d) Write the answer next to the **?**. *Circle the answer.*
(e) Complete the sentence.

Luis has ________ more boxes of football cards than baseball cards.

76. Aaron ran 7 laps of the track. Herme ran 15 laps of the track. What is the difference in the number of laps Aaron and Herme ran?

(a) Fill in the "who" and the "what."
(b) Write the numbers from the problem. Draw a bracket and a **?**.
(c) Solve the problem.
(d) Write the answer next to the **?**. *Circle the answer.*
(e) Complete the sentence.

Herme ran ________________________________ .

77. Woofy hid 5 bones in the backyard and Lassie hid 13 bones in the backyard. How many more bones did Lassie hide than Woofy?

(a) Fill in the "who" and the "what."
(b) Write the numbers from the problem. Draw a bracket and a **?**.
(c) Solve the problem.
(d) Write the answer next to the **?**. *Circle the answer.*
(e) Complete the sentence.

Lassie hid ________________________________ .

78. Popeye ate 13 cans of spinach. Sweet Pea ate 2 cans of spinach. What is the difference in the number of cans of spinach that Popeye and Sweet Pea ate?

(a) Fill in the "who" and the "what."
(b) Write the numbers from the problem. Draw a bracket and a **?**.
(c) Solve the problem.
(d) Write the answer next to the **?**. *Circle the answer.*
(e) Complete the sentence.

__________ | | | | | | | | | | | | | |

____

__________ | | |

____

____

Popeye ate ______ ______ cans of

____________________ than Sweet Pea.

6. Adding with the Continuous Model

79. Lacey picked 14 flowers. Lilly picked 16 flowers. When they put their flowers together to make a bouquet, how many flowers were in the bouquet?

(a) Fill in the blanks.
(b) Show your work.

Lacey's flowers ___

Lilly's flowers ___

? ___

The bouquet had ___ flowers.

80. Jana has 15 colored pencils at home and 10 colored pencils at school. How many colored pencils does Jana have in all?

(a) Draw unit bars of equal length.
(b) Write the numbers from the problem. Draw a bracket and a **?**.
(c) Solve the problem and fill in the blank after the equal sign.
(d) Write the answer next to the **?**. *Circle the answer.*
(e) Complete the sentence.

Jana's pencils at home

Jana's pencils at school

15 + 10 = ___

Jana has ___ colored pencils in all.

81. Anni put 12 boxes and 12 cans on the shelf. How many boxes and cans did Anni put on the shelf?

(a) Draw the unit bars.
(b) Write the numbers from the problem. Draw a bracket and a **?**.
(c) Solve the problem. Show your work.
(d) Write the answer next to the **?**. *Circle the answer.*
(e) Complete the sentence.

Anni's boxes

Anni's cans

Anni put ____ ____________ ______ ______ on the shelf.

82. Char bought 10 yards of orange cloth and 15 yards of blue cloth. How many yards of cloth did Char buy?

(a) Draw the unit bars.
(b) Write the numbers from the problem. Draw a bracket and a **?**.
(c) Solve the problem. Show your work.
(d) Write the answer next to the **?**. *Circle the answer.*
(e) Complete the sentence.

Char's orange cloth

Char's blue cloth

Char bought ___ yards of ____________.

83. At the fair, Tyrone sold 8 snow cones in the morning and 20 snow cones in the afternoon. How many snow cones did Tyrone sell?

(a) Draw the unit bars.
(b) Write the numbers from the problem. Draw a bracket and a **?**.
(c) Solve the problem. Show your work.
(d) Write the answer next to the **?**. *Circle the answer.*
(e) Complete the sentence.

Tyrone's morning
snow cones

Tyrone's afternoon
snow cones

Tyrone sold ___ ____________ ____________.

84. Alexa scored 12 points in the first half of the game and 18 points in the second half of the game. How many points did Alexa score?

(a) Draw the unit bars.
(b) Write the numbers from the problem. Draw a bracket and a **?**.
(c) Solve the problem. Show your work.
(d) Write the answer next to the **?**. *Circle the answer.*
(e) Complete the sentence.

Alexa's first-half points

Alexa's second-half points

Alexa scored ___ ____________.

85. Nidhi's cat weighs 5 pounds. Her dog weighs 11 pounds. When Nidhi picks up both of her pets at once, how much weight is she lifting?

(a) Draw the unit bars.
(b) Write the numbers from the problem. Draw a bracket and a **?**.
(c) Solve the problem. Show your work.
(d) Write the answer next to the **?**. *Circle the answer.*
(e) Complete the sentence.

Cat's weight

Dog's weight

Nidhi is lifting ______ ______________________ .

86. Samantha was at the beach. She collected 35 seashells and 20 sand dollars. How many seashells and sand dollars did she collect in all?

(a) Draw the unit bars.
(b) Write the numbers from the problem. Draw a bracket and a **?**.
(c) Solve the problem. Show your work.
(d) Write the answer next to the **?**. *Circle the answer.*
(e) Complete the sentence.

Samantha's seashells

Samantha's sand dollars

Samantha collected ___ seashells and sand dollars in all.

87. Ted has 20 apples, 30 pears, and 40 peaches in his store. How many pieces of fruit does he have?

(a) Draw the unit bars.
(b) Write the numbers from the problem. Draw a bracket and a **?**.
(c) Solve the problem. Show your work.
(d) Write the answer next to the **?**. *Circle the answer.*
(e) Complete the sentence.

Ted's apples

Ted's pears

Ted's peaches

Ted has _____ pieces of ____________________.

88. Erika counted 20 flamingos, 30 herons, and 25 ducks at the zoo. How many birds did she count in all?

(a) Draw the unit bars.
(b) Write the numbers from the problem. Draw a bracket and a **?**.
(c) Solve the problem. Show your work.
(d) Write the answer next to the **?**. *Circle the answer.*
(e) Complete the sentence.

Flamingos

Herons

Ducks

Erika counted ______ ____________________ in all.

7. Adding More of the Same Thing Using the Continuous Model

89. Tom had 55¢. His mom gave him 20¢ more. How much money does Tom have now?

(a) Draw the unit bars.
(b) Write the numbers from the problem. Draw a bracket and a **?**.
(c) Solve the problem. Show your work.
(d) Write the answer next to the **?**. *Circle the answer.*
(e) Complete the sentence.

Tom's money

Tom has ______ ____________________ .

90. Charles has 30 toy cars in one box, 25 cars in another box, and 35 cars in another box. How many cars does he have in all?

(a) Draw the unit bars.
(b) Write the numbers from the problem. Draw a bracket and a **?**.
(c) Solve the problem. Show your work.
(d) Write the answer next to the **?**. *Circle the answer.*
(e) Complete the sentence.

Charles's cars

Charles has ______ ____________________ in all.

91. The baker has 10 pounds of sugar in 1 bag, 25 pounds of sugar in another bag, and 25 pounds of sugar in the last bag. How many pounds of sugar does the baker have?

(a) Draw the unit bars.
(b) Write the numbers from the problem. Draw a bracket and a **?***.*
(c) Solve the problem. Show your work.
(d) Write the answer next to the **?***. Circle the answer.*
(e) Complete the sentence.

Baker's
sugar

The baker has ___ pounds of ______________________ .

92. Alexandra read 25 minutes on Monday, 25 minutes on Tuesday, and 50 minutes on Wednesday. How many total minutes did Alexandra read those 3 days?

(a) Draw the unit bars.
(b) Write the numbers from the problem. Draw a bracket and a **?***.*
(c) Solve the problem. Show your work.
(d) Write the answer next to the **?***. Circle the answer.*
(e) Complete the sentence.

Alexandra's
reading minutes

Alexandra read for ___ total ______________________ .

93. Sindhu strung 45 red beads and 20 blue beads on her necklace. How many beads did she use in all?

(a) Draw the unit bars.
(b) Write the numbers from the problem. Draw a bracket and a **?**.
(c) Solve the problem. Show your work.
(d) Write the answer next to the **?**. *Circle the answer.*
(e) Complete the sentence.

Sindhu's beads

Sindhu used _____ ____________________ in ____________ .

94. The farmer has 30 acres of corn and 40 acres of wheat. How many acres does he farm?

(a) Draw the unit bars.
(b) Write the numbers from the problem. Draw a bracket and a **?**.
(c) Solve the problem. Show your work.
(d) Write the answer next to the **?**. *Circle the answer.*
(e) Complete the sentence.

Farmer's acres

He farms _______ ____________________________ .

95. Suzi baked 18 chocolate cupcakes, 20 yellow cupcakes, and 30 white cupcakes. How many cupcakes did Suzi bake?

(a) Draw the unit bars.
(b) Write the numbers from the problem. Draw a bracket and a **?**.
(c) Solve the problem. Show your work.
(d) Write the answer next to the **?**. *Circle the answer.*
(e) Complete the sentence.

Suzi's cupcakes

Suzi baked ______ ______________________________ .

96. Keith stacked 25 newspapers in one pile, 25 newspapers in the second pile, and 30 newspapers in the last pile. How many newspapers did Keith stack?

(a) Draw the unit bars.
(b) Write the numbers from the problem. Draw a bracket and a **?**.
(c) Solve the problem. Show your work.
(d) Write the answer next to the **?**. *Circle the answer.*
(e) Complete the sentence.

Keith's piles of newspapers

Keith stacked ______ ______________________________ .

97. Carly painted 20 red chairs, 30 blue chairs, and 35 green chairs. How many chairs did she paint?

(a) Draw the unit bars.
(b) Write the numbers from the problem. Draw a bracket and a **?***.*
(c) Solve the problem. Show your work.
(d) Write the answer next to the **?***. Circle the answer.*
(e) Complete the sentence.

Carly's chairs

Carly painted ________ ________________________________ .

98. Devin had 28 red marbles, 30 blue marbles, and 42 purple marbles. He put all his marbles in a jar. How many marbles were in the jar?

(a) Fill in the "what."
(b) Draw the unit bars.
(c) Write the numbers from the problem. Draw a bracket and a **?***.*
(d) Solve the problem. Show your work.
(e) Write the answer next to the **?***. Circle the answer.*
(f) Complete the sentence.

Devin's _______________

There were _______ ________________ in the _______________.

99. Lydia has 50 green T-shirts, 33 red T-shirts, and 17 blue T-shirts in her store. How many T-shirts are in Lydia's store?

(a) Fill in the "what."
(b) Draw the unit bars.
(c) Write the numbers from the problem. Draw a bracket and a **?**.
(d) Solve the problem. Show your work.
(e) Write the answer next to the **?**. *Circle the answer.*
(f) Complete the sentence.

Lydia's ____________

There are ______ ________________________________ in

Lydia's ____________________ .

8. Subtracting with the Continuous Model

100. Jarod caught 9 crickets, but 3 jumped away. How many crickets did he have left?

(a) Solve the problem.
(b) Fill in the blanks.

Jarod's crickets

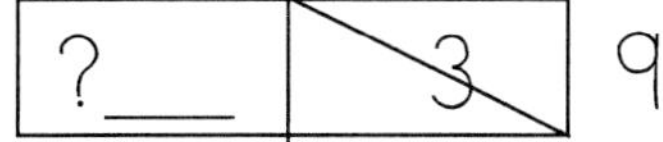

9 – 3 = ___

Jarod had ___ crickets left.

101. Rob brought a plate of 12 doughnuts to the party. His friends ate 8 doughnuts. How many doughnuts are on the plate now?

(a) Solve the problem.
(b) Fill in the blanks.

Rob's doughnuts

12 – 8 = ___

There are ______ ____________________ on the plate now.

102. Samuel had 12 glasses of lemonade. He sold 10 glasses. How many glasses were left?

(a) Solve the problem.
(b) Complete the sentence.

Samuel's glasses of lemonade

There were ___ glasses of ____________________ left.

103. Jenny had 12 pieces of chalk. Then 5 pieces broke. How many whole pieces of chalk does Jenny have now?

(a) Solve the problem.
(b) Complete the sentence.

Jenny's pieces of chalk

Jenny has ___ whole pieces of ________________ now.

104. Mei-Mei blew 13 bubbles, but 6 popped. How many bubbles are left?

(a) Solve the problem.
(b) Complete the sentence.

Mei-Mei's bubbles

There are ___ bubbles left.

105. Manny made 9 sandwiches. He sold 7. How many sandwiches are left to sell?

(a) Solve the problem.
(b) Complete the sentence.

Manny's sandwiches

There are _______ ___________________________ left to sell.

106. Grandma made 12 tarts. The children ate 4 of her tarts. How many tarts does Grandma have now?

(a) Solve the problem.
(b) Complete the sentence.

Grandma's tarts

Grandma has ___ tarts ___________.

107. Tracey had 9 key chains on her backpack. Then 6 key chains fell off. How many key chains does she have left?

(a) Solve the problem.
(b) Complete the sentence.

Tracey's key chains

Tracey has ___ key chains left.

108. The clown had 16 balloons, but 8 balloons popped. How many balloons does the clown have now?

(a) Solve the problem.
(b) Complete the sentence.

Clown's balloons

The clown has ___ balloons now.

109. Sam had 20 newspapers to sell. He sold 11. How many newspapers does he have left to sell?

(a) Solve the problem.
(b) Complete the sentence.

Sam's newspapers

Sam has ______________________________.

110. Mr. Yin grilled 30 hamburgers for the party. His friends ate 20 hamburgers. How many hamburgers were left?

(a) Solve the problem.
(b) Complete the sentence.

Mr. Yin's hamburgers

There were ______________________________ .

111. Mrs. Lopez had 40 bouquets at her store. She sold 20 bouquets by 10:00. How many bouquets were left after 10:00?

(a) Solve the problem.
(b) Complete the sentence.

Mrs. Lopez's bouquets

There were ______________________________

112. Jimmy had 50 quarters. He gave 25 quarters to his sister. How many quarters does he have now?

(a) Solve the problem.
(b) Complete the sentence.

Jimmy's quarters

Jimmy has ____ .

113. There were 75 frogs croaking near the pond. Then 25 of the frogs jumped into the water. How many frogs were left near the pond?

(a) Solve the problem.
(b) Complete the sentence.

Frogs

There were ____ .

114. There were 90 children in the cafeteria for lunch. Then 20 children finished and left for class. How many children were left in the cafeteria?

(a) Solve the problem.
(b) Complete the sentence.

Children in cafeteria

There were ______________________________.

115. Tarik had 100 peanuts in a bag. Then 50 peanuts spilled out. How many peanuts were left?

(a) Solve the problem.
(b) Complete the sentence.

Tarik's peanuts

There were ___ peanuts ______________________.

116. Mr. Singh had 100 lollipops for sale. He sold 95 lollipops. How many lollipops does he have now?

(a) Solve the problem.
(b) Complete the sentence.

Mr. Singh's lollipops

He now has ______________________________.

9. Sets of Numbers

117. There are 3 plates of cookies. Each plate has 4 cookies. How many cookies are there in all?

(a) Solve the problem.
(b) Fill in the blanks.

Plates of cookies 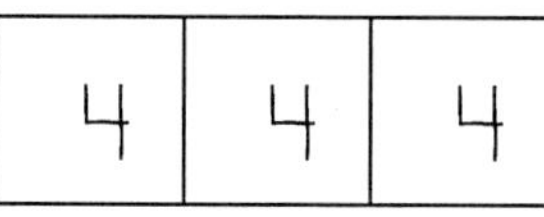 ? ___

$4 + 4 + 4 =$ ___

There are ___ cookies in all.

118. There were 4 birds' nests. Each nest had 3 eggs. How many eggs is that in all?

(a) Solve the problem.
(b) Complete the sentence.

Eggs in birds' nests

That is ______________________________.

119. Princess the cat had 3 litters of 5 kittens each. How many kittens did Princess have in all?

(a) Solve the problem.
(b) Complete the sentence.

Litters of kittens

Princess ________________________________ .

120. There were 6 children skating at the park. Each child wore 2 elbow pads. How many elbow pads did they have in all?

(a) Solve the problem.
(b) Complete the sentence.

Children's elbow pads

They had ________________________________ .

121. The 3 shelves in the ice cream store have 8 ice cream tubs on each shelf. How many ice cream tubs are on the 3 shelves?

(a) Solve the problem.
(b) Complete the sentence.

Ice cream

There are ______________________________ .

122. There were 5 carpenters. Each carpenter had 5 tools. How many tools is that in all?

(a) Solve the problem.
(b) Complete the sentence.

Carpenters' tools

That is ______________________________ .

123. There were 6 baskets. There were 3 pineapples in each basket. How many pineapples were in the 6 baskets?

(a) Solve the problem.
(b) Complete the sentence.

Baskets of pineapples

There were ______________________________ .

124. Eric can fit 6 pumpkins in his wagon. If Eric fills his wagon 4 times with pumpkins, how many pumpkins would that be in all?

(a) Solve the problem.
(b) Complete the sentence.

Eric's wagons of pumpkins

That would be ______________________________ .

125. There were 8 mules. Each mule carried 3 packs. How many packs did the 8 mules carry?

(a) Solve the problem.
(b) Complete the sentence.

Mules' packs

The 8 mules ______________________________ .

126. The cook placed 3 pancakes on each of 7 plates. How many pancakes would that be?

(a) Solve the problem.
(b) Complete the sentence.

Cook's plates of pancakes

That would be ______________________________ .

127. Sarah used 5 apples to make each pie. If she baked 6 pies, how many apples did she need?

(a) Solve the problem.
(b) Complete the sentence.

Sarah's apples in pies

Sarah needed ____________________________ .

128. Cupcakes are baked in batches of 12 cupcakes to a batch. If Sally put 3 batches of cupcakes in the oven, how many cupcakes did she bake?

(a) Solve the problem.
(b) Complete the sentence.

Sally's batches
of cupcakes

Sally baked____________________________ .

129. Polly, the parrot, loves sunflower seeds. She eats 10 seeds a day. How many seeds will Polly eat in 5 days?

(a) Solve the problem.
(b) Complete the sentence.

Polly's seeds

In 5 days Polly ______________________________ .

130. Alexandra put 10 gingerbread men in each box. There were 6 boxes of gingerbread men. How many gingerbread men were there in all?

(a) Solve the problem.
(b) Complete the sentence.

Alexandra's boxes
of gingerbread men

There were ______________________________ .